Marble-Step Meditations

Blessings From the Past

Winter Rand Forder

Parson's Porch Books

Marble-Step Meditations: Blessings from the Past
ISBN: Softcover 978-1-960326-47-8
Copyright © 2023 by Winter Rand Forder

Parson's Porch Books is an imprint of Parson's Porch & Company (PP&C) in Cleveland, Tennessee. PP&C is a self-funded charity which earns money by publishing books of noted authors, representing all genres. Its face and voice is **David Russell Tullock** who you can contact at: dtullock@parsonsporch.com.

Parson's Porch & Company *turns books into bread & milk* by sharing its profits with the poor.

www.parsonsporch.com

Marble-Step Meditations

Dedicated to JACK and PEYTON, our grandchildren, who are now in the process of making memories and have inspired me to remember my early years.

Acknowledgements

I want to express appreciation to my family for reading my manuscript and offering helpful suggestions. Most of all, I want to thank each one of them for their love and encouragement:

> Anne, my wife;
> Brad, my son, and Caitlin, my daughter-in-law;
> Elizabeth, my daughter, and Seth, my son-in-law.

They are all personal blessings in my life, and I thank God for them each day. I am grateful to William Tuck, a friend and gifted minister, for his guidance. My special thanks to Brad Forder for his work in organizing and formatting.

Contents

"The lines have fallen for me in pleasant places; yea, I have a goodly heritage."

(Psalm 16:6, R.S.V.)

Introduction

GOING HOME AGAIN

The first seven years of my life, 1945-1952, my family lived in a row house with white marble steps on Dukeland Street in the city of Baltimore, Maryland.

Aubrey Bodine, a photojournalist, wrote, "The white marble steps of Baltimore have become the city's trademark and a marvel to visitors. Most of them are white marble, from nearby quarries, and housewives vie in keeping them bright. In any block, there is seldom a day that someone is not out scrubbing them."[1]

For me, those marble steps are symbolic of my entrance into a life in which family, faith, virtues, church, values, and friendships were essentials. As I reflect on those early years around the marble steps, the memories help me to recognize blessings of which I was unaware at the time.

---

[1] A. Aubrey Bodine, My Maryland, (Baltimore, Maryland: Camera Magazine, 1952), p. 51.

Frederick Buechner once commented, "'For all thy blessings, known and unknown, remembered and forgotten, we give thee thanks,' runs an old prayer, and it is for the all but unknown ones and the more than half-forgotten ones that we do well to look back over the journeys of our lives, because it is their presence that makes the life of each of us a sacred journey."[2]

In 1983, after attending a meeting in Baltimore, I decided to visit the old neighborhood. It had been thirty years since my family and I had moved from Dukeland Street to a house on Gwynn Oak Avenue. I was curious about my childhood home.

When I drove to Dukeland Street and turned onto our block, I could immediately see the changes. I arrived in front of 610 Dukeland Street. I stopped my car and stayed inside of the vehicle. As I surveyed the property, I noticed that the row house looked smaller than I had remembered. Plywood had been placed over the windows, and the glass in the front door had been broken and poorly repaired. The white marble steps were filthy and appeared as if they

---

[2] Frederick Buechner, Listening to Your Life, (New York: Harper Collins, 1992), p. 9.

had not been scrubbed recently. Of course, the family members I loved and who loved me were no longer there.

After some sad moments, I drove to my home in Easton, Maryland, where my wife and children were waiting for me. Perhaps Thomas Wolfe was right, You Can't Go Home Again, as the title of his book correctly expresses my experience.

However, in the meditations which I included in this book, I have attempted "going home again" another way. The good and bad memories we have made in our childhood homes continue to influence us throughout our lives.

We all are responsible for our decisions and actions and reactions in various situations. Prayerfully, in our backgrounds, though, there are beliefs, attitudes, and values which can become blessings as we grow. Many parents are comforted and challenged by Solomon's wisdom, "Train up a child in the way he should go, and when he is old he will not depart from it" (Proverbs 22: 6).

"Going home again" in that way, we can be recipients of blessings, "half-forgotten" and "unknown." My prayer is that the following meditations will provide a glimpse into my early years and also a challenge for others to remember blessings from the past.

Chapter 1:

THE GOOD DOCTOR

Dr. Zepp climbed the marble steps to enter the front door of the house. He was the first physician I encountered in my life. He always came to our house to treat me for illnesses and to give me needed shots and vaccinations.

Dr. Zepp became my friend. We eventually had nicknames for each other. I called him "Eddie," and he called me "Charlie." Since my family did not own an automobile, I was fascinated by his big Buick. One day he asked my mother if he could take me for a ride around the block in that car. What a thrill it was for me to have that opportunity!

He was a busy professional who took the time to befriend a little boy who admired him. In addition to his medical skill, Dr. Zepp possessed a compassion, which was an important factor in the healing process.

I appreciated a story told by the speaker at a graduation ceremony for nursing students. She said that Alan Alda, who played the character of "Hawkeye Pierce," a physician on the television series, "M*A*S*H," was asked one year to give the commencement address at the Columbia University Medical School graduation. He advised the graduates to remember as they treated their patients that "the head bone is connected to the heart bone." We know that is bad anatomy, but it does lead to excellent medical care.

Dr. Zepp was a good example of a physician whose caring ways helped the healing process.

I am reminded of another good doctor. He wrote the Gospel of Luke and the Book of Acts in the New Testament. It reveals his gracious character that he never identified himself as the writer of the Gospel or Acts. Luke was called "the beloved physician" (Colossians 4:14), and he told the good news of Jesus, "the Great Physician." Jesus went about doing good. His compassion was evident. Children were drawn to Him. He reached out to all people and brought healing to many hurting individuals.

On my visits to the Johns Hopkins Hospital in Baltimore, Maryland, I have always been touched by the marble statue of "Christ, the Divine Healer," which is situated under the dome in the lobby. It is a replica of a statue by the Danish sculptor, Bertel Thorwaldsen. It portrays the risen Christ with open arms and nail prints in his hands and feet. The caring figure seems to be offering comfort and hope as persons with various needs enter or leave the hospital. The inscription at the base of the statue conveys the message, "Come unto me, all ye that are weary and heavy laden, and I will give you rest" (Matthew 11:28).

Dr. Zepp climbing the marble steps of our house has become a sacred memory, which has awakened me to the blessed friendship with the Great Physician today.

Chapter 2:

NEIGHBORS AND FENCES

Marble steps often served as front porches for the residents of row houses. Neighbors would sit on the steps and visit with neighbors. At that time in my life, every day in the neighborhood was "a beautiful day in the neighborhood"- to quote the words of a song by Mr. Fred Rogers.

The family next to us were good neighbors. A four-year-old boy and a five-year- old girl often played in the backyard of their house. And, at three years old, I played in our yard. We showed each other our toys and raced with brooms on our stick horses. Those yards were narrow, with wire fences which surrounded each yard, and gates which led into an alley.

One day, the boy next door and I were talking through the fence, and his sister came out of the house. She approached us and motioned for me to come closer to the fence. I thought she was going to give me something or tell me a secret. Instead, she "planted" a kiss on me through that wire fence. I was dumbfounded and confused.

My first kiss and even from an older woman! Several days later, her mother told my mother that the girl had been diagnosed with measles. A few days later, I started with the measles. I have discovered that it is not merely good fences that make good neighbors!

The Gospel of Luke (10:25-37, GNT), describes the day when Jesus told the truth about being a good neighbor. A teacher of the religious law asked Jesus a question about eternal life, and then Jesus countered with a question about the answer given in the Scriptures. The man responded, "'Love the Lord your God with all your heart, with all your soul, with all your strength, and with all your mind;' and 'Love your neighbor as you love yourself.'" Jesus approved of the teacher's answer and told him, "do this and you will live." However, the man continued to try to trap Jesus with the question, "Who is my neighbor?" Responding, Jesus told a story which contained a challenge.

Jesus said a man was robbed and severely beaten as he traveled from Jerusalem to Jericho. Two religious leaders saw the injured man but did not help him. Then a Samaritan, who would have been despised by the listener, stopped, bandaged the man's wounds, transported him to an inn, and provided for his continuing care there. Jesus asked the religious teacher to consider the three persons who encountered the beaten man and to identify the neighbor. Without mentioning the name, "Samaritan," the religious expert replied, "The one who was kind to him." Jesus' challenge was, "You go, then, and do the same." We are left wondering if he ever did!

Jesus' story prompts me to wonder about my own compassion. Whose neighbor am I? And how big is my neighborhood? My compassion should reach beyond the area where I live. My compassion should knock down the fences built to exclude others. Wherever there is a need, I should have the courage to reach out and care. Then, it will indeed be "a beautiful day in God's neighborhood."

Chapter 3:

THE COAL CONNECTION

Located in the front of our row house, next to the marble steps, was a window which led into the cellar. Below the window in the cellar was a large coal bin.

At certain times a coal truck would park in front of the house, lower a metal slide, and position it through the open window. Then the coal would flow from the truck into that coal bin in the cellar. During the cold winter months, my parents would shovel coal from the bin into the furnace. Thereby, we would have heat in the house.

Disobeying my parents, I would sometimes wander into that coal bin and play. My parents would then have to dust me off, clean me up, and order me not to play in there. Also, there were consequences for my disobedience!

There are two lessons I have learned from my limited experience with that coal. First, coal was a resource we needed to provide warmth and comfort during the cold weather. I am reminded of the inner resources we need in our lives to sustain us during tough times. We need to sense the warmth of God's presence through the ups and downs of our lives. And in order to do so, we must be prepared.

The apostle Paul once advised his young son in the faith Timothy, "Physical fitness is quite valuable, but spiritual fitness is worth more than anything, because it enables one to have life for both the present and the future,"(1 Timothy 4:8, Clarence Jordan's Translation).

In preparation, those spiritual exercises can include: Bible reading and study, prayer, worship, and constant gratitude for God's grace. Those disciplines can help us to build up our spiritual muscles, so that resources will be available for the stormy blast.

There is a second lesson that emerges from my playing in the coal dust and dirt. I often looked like "Pig-Pen," the character in the "Peanuts" comic strip, when I came out of that coal bin.

In the rough and tumble of everyday life, we collect and accumulate attitudes and actions which color our relationships with God and with our fellow human beings. We need help and forgiveness to "clean up our act." In Psalm 51, we read David's prayer, "Have mercy on me, O God, according to thy steadfast love; according to thy abundant mercy blot out my transgressions. Wash me thoroughly from my iniquity and cleanse me from my sin!" (verses 1-2, RSV).

God has provided that forgiveness through the life, death, and resurrection of Jesus Christ. Through confession, repentance, and faith in Him, we can discover that cleansing. The writer of the book of Hebrews encourages us, "let us lay aside every weight and sin which clings so closely, and let us run with perseverance the race that is set before us, looking to Jesus the pioneer and perfecter of our faith….," (Hebrews 12:1b-2a, RSV).

That coal connection has reminded me of lessons about comfort and newness of life. God is always available to provide us with the help we need.

Chapter 4:

A LOST FOOTBALL

Through my father's influence, baseball became my favorite sport. Although I was not as interested in football, I had a football which I kicked and tossed in the backyard of our row house with the white marble steps. I remember going with my mother to visit Uncle Bob and Aunt Edna, who lived just a few blocks from us. Uncle Bob was my grandmother's brother. On one visit, he was watching television. The University of Maryland was playing football, and he became so excited when the Terps scored a touchdown and so disgusted when they fumbled the ball. He talked to the television set throughout the game!

At home, I played with my football. One day, when I had finished playing, I left my football outside in our yard. The next day I looked for the football everywhere in our small yard, and it was not there. I was upset. I continued to look in our yard and even in the alley behind our house, but I never found my football. Grief and betrayal emerged for the first time in my young life. My loving grandmother understood my confused feelings, took me by the hand, and walked with me to a store where she bought me another football. I was a happy three-year-old boy! I learned that there can be life beyond loss.

Religious leaders had been criticizing Jesus for spending time and having table fellowship with persons they considered to be outcasts. Jesus then told the stories about a lost sheep, a lost coin, and two lost sons. In all three instances, there was something lost. However, after considerable, careful searching, that which was lost was found.

One sheep was missing from its place in the flock of one hundred. The concerned shepherd left the ninety-nine and searched for that one sheep until he found it. He then carried it home and called friends and neighbors together for a celebration. He said, "I am so happy I found my lost sheep. Let us celebrate!" (Luke 15: 6, GNT). Jesus then emphasized the joy of a loving God over a lost person who returns to his or her place in close relationship with Him. The religious leaders were missing that personal experience.

A woman lost a valuable coin. She then searched every area of her house until she finally found it. She called her friends and neighbors together and said, "I am so happy I found the coin I lost. Let us celebrate!" (Luke 15: 9, GNT). Again, Jesus pointed to God's joy and love and the personal fellowship those self-righteous leaders were missing.

A loving father had two sons who both were lost (Luke 15: 11- 32). One left his rightful place in the family to travel to a far country. He experienced hard times because of that separation. He finally recognized how lost he had been, and turned toward home. Before he reached the property, his loving father ran out to meet him, hugged him, kissed him, and restored him to his rightful place in the family. The other son, even though he lived right there and worked hard on the premises, remained separated from his brother. The loving father went to him and begged him to come and join the joyous occasion, but we are left wondering if he ever returned to his important place with the father in the family circle.

I remember the time when I lost my football, and even though it was never found, I was thankful for the caring action of my grandmother. She went out of her way to help me experience a joy that superseded the sadness and grief. Through it all, I have been led to believe in the loving, joyful, seeking God who has come to us in Jesus to make possible life-affirming rescues.

Chapter 5:

GOOD HUMOR

We could hear the ringing of the bell on the truck when it was a block away. There was excitement in the neighborhood. Hearing that sound, parents and children hurried outside, walked down the marble steps of their row houses, stood on the sidewalk, and waited.

Soon the bell ringing grew louder, and the truck moved onto our street. It was a white, refrigerated truck with the words, "Good Humor," painted on the side. Also, there was a picture of ice cream on a stick under those words. The truck stopped in the middle of our block.

My parents had given me a nickel to spend. I usually asked the driver of the truck for a popsicle or a fudgesicle and then handed him my five cents. He was always dressed in a white suit and wore a white cap. He smiled at us customers and always seemed to live up to the name on his truck, "Good Humor." The ice cream treat was delightful, but that "good-natured" man, with the smile on his face, was the center of everyone's attention. Furthermore, his radiant personality was contagious.

Jesus once said to his followers, who were gathered around him, "be of good cheer" (John16:33b, RSV). He certainly enjoyed laughter and smiles and a good-natured attitude, as do most persons. However, he also knew about the reality of sadness and difficulty and pain. Preceding his words about "being of good cheer," he said, "In the world you have tribulation." He was sharing with his disciples that when trouble comes, as it always does, they should not lose heart. And then, he gave the reason they could walk on, through it all, with "good cheer." He made the impossible possible by providing a higher level of living through his victory over death, evil, and sin. He explained, "I have overcome the world."

The apostle Paul was a good example of that victorious living. At a particular time in his life, he had every reason to be negative and sad and discouraged and miserable. He was confined in a Roman prison, and he had been used to travel and adventures throughout the Mediterranean world. As his freedom of movement was taken away from him, he had time to reflect on his past and regret his hatred of others and his rebellion against God. Also, he had time to worry about the future and his possible execution. In addition, he suffered from a "thorn in the flesh," a physical ailment which caused him pain and discomfort. He had many reasons to lose heart. In spite of all that trouble, he communicated a positive outlook, "I am ready for anything through the strength of the one who lives within me" (Philippians 4:13, J.B. Phillips' Translation). The indwelling presence and power of Christ was the source of his "good cheer." Christ continues to be the Source of the "good cheer" that is so desperately needed every day in our corners of the world.

I hope that the "Good Humor" man who drove his truck to our neighborhood every week knew that truth. I imagine that he must have had some bad days: when his truck had a flat tire, or when he had to deal with cantankerous customers, or when he was not feeling well. Since we always noticed his smile and experienced his radiant personality, I believe he knew well the True Source of that "Good Humor."

Chapter 6:

CLOSE-UP HEROES

He would come out of the row house which was directly across from our house, walk down the marble steps, and climb onto the fire truck. As the truck, with flashing lights, moved away, and turned the corner, the siren could be heard on the busy highway.

Our neighbor was a firefighter in the Baltimore City Fire Department. I learned that those firemen hurried to extinguish fires and rescue people. They were called on day or night to respond to many dangerous situations. Unselfishly, they risked their lives to save the lives of other persons. They were heroes.

As a child, I had heroes in the sports world. Yogi Berra, Ted Williams, and Stan Musial were famous baseball stars. I also had heroes in the entertainment world. I was thrilled by the adventures of cowboys like, Hopalong Cassidy, Roy Rogers, and Gene Autry. However, I had never met those individuals. They were long-distance heroes.

Our fireman-neighbor was someone I knew. He was a close-up hero. And I have discovered through the years that I had many close-up heroes who helped me and inspired me and served as role models.

I think of some family members, church leaders, and Sunday school teachers. When I reached school age, I remember teachers and professors who were interested not only in their subject matter but also in their students. They all went "the second mile" to inspire youth and help us to learn and grow.

The close-up hero I admired and respected and loved the most was my father. He was a "tall soul," spiritually, mentally, socially, and physically. His compassion and integrity were noteworthy. He was never too busy to spend time with me. For example, after a hard day's work, he would often grab a baseball bat, glove, and tennis ball, take me by the hand, and walk with me to a nearby sandlot. There I learned about throwing, catching, and hitting a baseball. But greater than merely the sport of baseball, every day, through word and deed, he shared with me the values that were essential for a meaningful life. His Christian faith "rang true" in all situations and circumstances. He was committed to following Jesus.

Jesus once spoke of what was necessary to become one of his followers. He said, "If you want to come with me, you must forget yourself, take up your cross every day, and follow me" (Luke 9:23, GNT). His journey led to and beyond a cross, through which he made it possible for us to experience abundant and eternal life. As we attempt to walk his way, he has promised to be with us always. (Matthew 28:20).

Where have all the heroes gone? Perhaps we need to recognize that a close-up hero is beside us every day.

Chapter 7:

THE PIANO BENCH

When people walked up the marble steps of our row house and entered, they were in a vestibule. To the left was our living room, and the largest piece of furniture in the living room was the piano. There was a wooden piano bench, and on the seat of the bench was a small Persian rug.

Many times, the family would gather around that piano and sing as my mother played hymns and popular songs. She was an excellent pianist. She taught piano lessons, played the piano in church worship services, and for several years served as the church organist and choir director at a church in Baltimore. Music was one way my mother expressed her Christian faith. "Jesus Loves Me" was one of the first songs she taught me. The truth of that song is the foundation of my faith today.

I have many good memories of the central place that piano and that bench held in our home. However, there is one bad memory of my close encounter with the piano bench. It is a vivid memory.

One day, when I was four years old, I tripped in the living room and fell face first into that bench. I knocked out my four front teeth. The dentist advised my parents that the remaining pieces of the teeth needed to be removed to make room for the growth of my permanent teeth. An appointment was made with an oral surgeon, and I remember well the day I had that surgery. My parents went with me to the office in downtown Baltimore. After I was settled in the room, the dentist and nurses put a gas mask over my face to put me to sleep. Then, with the pain and the resulting empty place in my mouth, it took time to recover. My recovery was made easier by the good care and help I received from family and medical personnel.

After that episode, I tried to avoid the piano bench. Perhaps that is one reason I was not interested in sitting on any piano bench to learn to play the piano!

As we remember the past, some memories provide us with comfort and inspiration and encouragement. Other memories can lead to fear or regret or pain. For me, that bench is symbolic of both singing and stumbling. If I so choose, I can learn lessons from both.

In terms of the Christian faith, for example, I believe that the compassionate Christ shows us that God is there to rejoice with us when we sing and to weep with us when we stumble and fall. God's love is deep enough and high enough and wide enough and long enough to remember us at all times. The call for us is to remember Him and His presence with us through all our experiences.

Throughout the Bible, we can read the truth. Moses told the people of Israel not to forget God because God had remembered them in the good times and in the tough times (Deuteronomy 8:11-20). At the Last Supper, in the Upper Room, Jesus broke bread and took the cup of wine and said, "Do this in remembrance of me" (1 Corinthians 11:24-25). Those symbols point us to his death on the cross, where the love of God for us was given ultimate expression. After the cross, the resurrection of Christ assures us of the living presence of God at all times. How could we ever forget the God who remembers us with such sacrificial love? How could we ever forget, even through the stumbling times, "Jesus loves me! This I know, For the Bible tells me so . . . "?

Chapter 8:

A DROOPY HORSE

The marble steps led to the front door of our row house. At the back of the house was a narrow yard. A fence enclosed the yard, with a gate leading into an alley. The alley was busy with delivery trucks coming and going to the back door of a bakery, which was located across the alley from us. My parents forbid me from opening the gate and going into the alley, but I did stand in the yard and watch all the activity.

Frequently, a horse-drawn wagon would move through the alley. The driver would announce, "melons, cantaloupes, tomatoes, and corn," as he continued to move along. The wagon was filled with vegetables and fruit, but I never remember anyone in our neighborhood stopping the wagon and buying any of the produce.

My attention was usually focused on the horse that pulled the wagon. The horse, with blinders on each side of its head, appeared to be so weary and droopy as it moved slowly in the alley. I felt sorry for that animal. I had seen photos of horses which raced at Pimlico Race Track in our city. Several times, I had seen Baltimore City Police Officers riding horses in the downtown area. However, I had never seen a horse in such poor condition as the one pulling that heavy load.

Reflecting on that scene, I now realize that I had overlooked the person driving the wagon. He also appeared to be droopy and weary and poor. He was trying hard to make a living, but didn't seem to be doing well. The man was tired.

Many persons today can identify with that man. They are using the resources they have at their disposal to deal with heavy loads, and they are weary and worn. They need help in coping with illnesses, family difficulties, financial problems, grief, loneliness, and many other burdens.

Jesus once invited weary, droopy individuals to come to him for rest. He said, "Come to me, all who labor and are heavy laden, and I will give you rest" (Matthew 11: 28, RSV). When we respond to his invitation, those weighty loads do not automatically disappear, but he provides us with the strength we need to stand up straight and to keep going.

Also, "the essence of the Christian life is to shoulder the loads of one another" (Galatians 6: 2, Clarence Jordan's Translation). Followers of Jesus Christ need to be alert and available to help carry the weight of that which is wearing others down and out.

Perhaps, if the tired man on the wagon had been receptive to Jesus' invitation through the effort of a sensitive, compassionate, follower of Jesus, the droopy horse might have sensed the positive difference and responded accordingly.

Chapter 9:

LET'S TALK

In the row house with the marble steps, the telephone was situated on a table between the living room and the dining room. At that time, telephones did not have buttons to push or dials to turn. To make a call, the caller would pick up the receiver, and an operator would then say, "Operator. Number, please." The caller would give the telephone number to the operator, who would connect the call.

As a preschooler, I would sometimes pick up the receiver, hear the voice of the operator, and try to talk with her. My parents and the operator were not pleased! I was also curious about "the party line," to which we were connected. Sometimes, when we picked up the receiver to make a call, a conversation could be heard between people we did not know. I learned that we were not supposed to listen but to hang up the phone and wait until the line was clear to make our calls.

Conversations were important in our home. On special occasions, when our extended family gathered, relatives would sit around the dining room table for hours and talk, and listen, and laugh, and argue. I learned early in my life the value of those sharing times.

Jesus engaged in many conversations as he gave the time to focus on every person that he met. For example, in the city of Jerusalem, a religious leader came to Jesus with some big questions. As the conversation unfolded, Jesus introduced him to the need and the significance of a new birth. Through the discussion, Nicodemus encountered the Truth in the person of this Jesus (John 3: 1ff).

One day, as Jesus was passing through Samaria, he stopped in the town of Sychar and sat down by a well. A Samaritan woman came to that well to draw water, and an unlikely conversation took place. Moving through the different levels of the woman's understanding, Jesus offered her life-giving water. She then left her water jar at the well and rushed into town to tell people that this Jesus just might be the Savior, for whom they had been waiting. As a result, many people did believe in him.

Whether Jesus was in the important city of Jerusalem or the little, Samaritan town of

Sychar, he took the time to listen to the lives of individuals and then to share with them his saving power. Those conversations revealed to others that he was the Truth.

As the Truth, his practice of prayer was the ultimate conversation. His relationship with the Father God involved talking and listening. Teaching his followers to pray, "Our Father who art in heaven" (Matthew 6: 9), Jesus opened the way for us to talk with God anywhere, at any time, about anything. In our conversations with God, we also need to listen. In the Garden of Gethsemane, Jesus struggled in prayer as he approached the Father God three times and waited for an answer, "My Father, if it is possible, take this cup of suffering from me! Yet not what I want, but what you want" (Matthew 26: 39, GNT). The answer came, and Jesus endured a cross, followed by the resurrection and the hope we can claim through him. As we often struggle in prayer, God is seeking to communicate with us in various ways: through the Bible, through other persons, through happenings in our lives, through His creation, and through other means. We can be open and alert and respond as did Samuel, "Speak, for thy servant hears" (Samuel 3: 10b, RSV).

Chapter 10:

THE LITTLE RED ROCKING CHAIR

The little red rocking chair was situated in the living room. It was the perfect fit for my height and weight. At three, four, and five years old, I would sometimes rock fast, or throw my legs over the side, or try to fall over backwards. One time, I got a pencil and poked four holes in the leather of one of the arms. I did indeed abuse that little chair!

There were other times, though, when I just sat in the chair and looked out our front window. I saw the marble steps and the sidewalk and the street. I watched people walk past our house and cars move through the neighborhood. At different times of the year, I noticed white clouds moving in the blue sky or birds flying or rain falling or snow landing on the ground. If anyone came to the front door, I recognized relatives but wondered about strangers. I really did enjoy those moments of sitting still and looking outside.

I was especially thrilled, though, when I could go outside. My parents would carry my tricycle out the front door and put it on the sidewalk. I would then ride many times to the end of our block and back to our house. I was excited to be on the move. There were times when I fell off my bike and skinned my knee. After stopping to get medicine and a bandage and to dry the tears, I got back on my bike and continued to pedal fast. The little red rocking chair was good for sitting and for getting up to go outside. The Christian life consists of both times to sit and also times to get up and go and do. It is not merely a spectator religion, and it is not just a do-gooder club.

Psalm 46 describes the active presence of God in His world and declares His message to us, "Be still, and know that I am God" (vs. 10a, RSV). James, a leader in the early church, continues the thought by telling his fellow believers not only to sit and look and listen, but also to put the truth they have witnessed into practice, "But be doers of the word, and not hearers only, deceiving yourselves" (James 1: 22, RSV).

Jesus was very active and involved in human life, as he taught and preached and healed and cast out demons. His compassion was evident, and he helped many persons, regardless of their status in society, to recognize the love of God. In the middle of all that activity, we learn that he would often take time to be still and pray. Before choosing the twelve disciples, he prayed all night. That quiet time away from his crowded days was essential as he then continued to go and do.

A rich young man approached Jesus one day and asked him what he needed to do to inherit eternal life. Jesus recognized that this outstanding individual had learned well the commandments. He must have sat at the feet of some good teachers. With love for this person, Jesus explained to him that he then needed to get up from his seat of learning and take action, "Go…sell…give…come…follow…" (Mark 10: 21). The sad commentary is that the rich young man turned away from the Truth.

I pray that good memories of that little red rocking chair will always inspire me both to deepen my faith by sitting still and also to widen my faith by going and doing.

Chapter 11

STREETCARS

Riding on streetcars was a memorable part of my early years. Leaving the marble steps, my parents and I walked two blocks on Dukeland Street to Edmondson Avenue, and waited at marked stops for the streetcars.

The streetcars were electric, moving on tracks embedded in the streets, and powered by overhead wires. A number designating the specific route and the name of the destination were on the front of the streetcar. Names such as: Garrison Boulevard, Walbrook Junction, Camden Station, Woodlawn, and others, were familiar.

The streetcar stopped, and the motorman opened the front door and the side door for passengers to enter and to exit. My memories include, the motormen wearing uniforms, the receptacles in which passengers deposited coins for the ride, the panel of buttons and switches used to drive the streetcar, the tokens, and the transfers. I especially remember the crowd of passengers.

Sometimes, I was able to sit on a seat next to my mother or father. Many times, though, I had to sit next to someone I did not know, while one of my parents sat on a seat across the aisle beside someone they did not know. When the streetcar was very crowded, I had to stand in the aisle next to my father. I felt so small in the middle of that crowd. However, my father held on to a leather strap hanging from the ceiling, and I held tightly to his hand.

During those streetcar rides, I observed persons of different ages, races, and attitudes. It was a good introduction for me to the world I would experience in later years. When I was school age, my parents taught me through word and deed to be respectful of all persons. For example, when I was seated on a crowded streetcar, and I noticed a person who was having difficulty standing in the aisle, I learned to get up and offer her or him my seat.

Jesus was often surrounded by a crowd. Crowds of people followed him from place to place. In the middle of the crowd, he taught, preached Good News about the kingdom of God, and healed many persons of diseases and disabilities. His compassion was evident. He recognized their helplessness and regarded them as "sheep without a shepherd" (Matthew 9: 35-36). For example, his heart-felt concern for them was expressed when he provided food for thousands of hungry men, women, and children (Matthew 14: 13-21; Matthew 15: 32-39).

When Jesus witnessed the crowds, he never saw a mob or a throng. He always focused on the persons in those groups. Individuals mattered. One day in the crowd around Jesus, a woman who had been ill for twelve years touched the edge of his cloak and was healed. Jesus asked, "Who touched me?" Everyone else saw only the crowd. Jesus, though, recognized that personal touch. When the woman finally identified herself, Jesus affirmed her faith and emphasized how valuable she really was, "My daughter, your faith has made you well. Go in peace" (Luke 8: 42-48).

Whenever we feel lost in the middle of the crowd, the Christian faith assures each one of us that God, Who has come to us in Jesus Christ, reaches through the throng and with His touch of love, brings us to the front, and includes us in the family circle.

Sometimes feeling small in our crowded world today, I reflect on those moments when I was a preschooler standing in the aisle of a crowded streetcar. I was surrounded by persons who were larger than I. Through it all, I was able to stand tall because I held tightly to my father's hand. Just so, the strong presence of the Father God makes it possible for us to stand tall in the middle of today's crowd.

Chapter 12

A BEGINNER

Church was always a vital part of the life of our family. We attended and participated in the activities of the Temple Baptist Church in the Walbrook area. Members of our extended family also participated in various aspects of the ministry of that church.

Since we did not own an automobile, when we stepped down the marble steps of our house to go to the church, we often walked to the closest streetcar stop and rode on streetcars to church. Sometimes we were given rides in the cars of family members or friends.

My earliest memories of church are from my attendance in the Beginners' Sunday School department. Miss Rose was our teacher and was a loving soul. She communicated the love of Jesus to us little ones through the sound of her voice, her facial expressions, and her encouragement. When she told us stories from the Bible, she always mentioned the name, "Jesus," with reverence. I remember a picture which hung on the wall in our classroom. It depicted Jesus as a shepherd, who was caring for his sheep. With the memory of that picture in my mind, I am not surprised that I have always appreciated William Blake's poem, "The Lamb."

> Little lamb, who made thee?
> Dost thou know who made thee?
> Gave thee life and bade thee feed
> By the stream and o'er the mead;
> Gave thee clothing of delight,
> Softest clothing, woolly bright;
> Gave thee such a tender voice,
> Making all the vales rejoice?
> Little lamb, who made thee?
> Dost thou know who made thee?
> Little lamb, I'll tell thee;
> Little lamb, I'll tell thee;
> He is called by thy name,
> For he calls himself a lamb,
> He is meek and he is mild,
> He became a little child, -
> I a child and thou a lamb,
> We are called by his name.
> Little lamb, God bless thee!
> Little lamb, God bless thee![3]

---

[3] Caroline Miles Hill, ed. The World's Great Religious Poetry, (New York: The Macmillan Company, 1924), p. 264.

As I consider my journey in the Christian faith, I am convinced that I am still a "beginner." The older I become, the more questions I have about faith's ups and downs. The older I become, the more I realize that I have a long way to grow. When we follow Jesus, we continue throughout our lives to learn, for we are disciples. Disciples are students or apprentices. In the Sermon on the Mount, Jesus taught, "You are to be perfect, like your Heavenly Father" (Matthew 5: 48, J.B. Phillips' Translation). The goal has been set for us. We never reach that goal, but it continues to be there to challenge us to stretch and grow. Whether we are preschoolers or senior citizens, we need to keep striving "to win the prize, which is God's call through Christ Jesus to the life above" (Philippians 3: 12-14, GNT).

The twelve disciples, who were called by Jesus, listened to his teachings. They watched him when he prayed, healed diseases, freed demon-possessed individuals, calmed storms, and performed many wondrous acts of love. He once sent them on a mission and gave them authority and power to preach the Kingdom of God, to cure diseases, and to drive out demons. The disciples were experienced followers of Jesus. As Jesus faced death on the cross, he attempted to prepare them for that ordeal. It is significant that he still referred to them as "My children" (John 13: 33). He gave them "a new commandment" (John 13: 34), which brought them back to basics; to love one another as he had loved them. That was the badge of their discipleship. They were still "beginners" in the matter of learning about love.

It is a blessing to be called "a child of God." Each one of us matters. God loves us and wants the best for our lives. Jesus tried to make that clear. Throughout the journey of life, God is with us and for us. We still need to learn to share that unconditional love.

I am grateful to Miss Rose, who demonstrated the significance of being a "beginner" then and now.

Chapter 13

WALK WITH ME

I did not learn to walk until after my first birthday. One day my aunt held out her hands and encouraged me to take some steps toward her. I let go of what I was grasping and walked for the first time. After that accomplishment, I was on the move, and when I stumbled and fell, I knew that I could get up and continue walking.

When I was an infant, my parents carried me up and down the marble steps at the front of our house. As I learned to walk, they took my hand and steadied me on those steps. It was not long before I was able and anxious to walk up and down those steps by myself.

Walking was part of my family's daily routine. We walked to grocery stores, pharmacies, relatives' houses, streetcar stops, playgrounds, shops, and other places. Walking is good exercise and can provide persons with a healthy perspective.

Jesus was at home in the created world around him. As he walked along, he noticed flowers growing, birds flying, farmers sowing seed, fig trees withering, and so much more. He was never too busy to pay attention to needy individuals. In those walks, he never treated them as interruptions. On the way to the city of Jericho, Jesus stopped walking and approached a blind beggar sitting on the side of the road and calling out to Jesus. Even though his followers objected, he took the time to heal that individual, whom he considered to be important. Then, in the city of Jericho, he stopped walking and took time to visit with a rich, successful man, named Zacchaeus. Salvation was the result, and Zacchaeus' life was changed. Jesus walked, and as he did, he looked and listened and often stopped.

God has come to walk with us in the person of Jesus Christ and calls us to walk in fellowship with Him. It takes faith on our part to respond. We let go of the superficial props which support us, and let God be our source of strength.

The prophet Isaiah declared that "those who trust in the Lord for help will find their strength renewed. They will rise on wings like eagles; they will run and not get weary; they will walk and not grow weak" (Isaiah 40: 31, GNT).

The apostle Paul explained to the church in Corinth, "We walk by faith, not by sight" (2 Corinthians 5: 7, R.S.V.). He knew that to be true from his personal experience of conversion on the road to Damascus (Acts 9).

Every day we all are learning to walk with God. Sometimes we stumble and fall. Sometimes we lose our way. Through it all, the Good News continues to be that we can take hold of God's outstretched hand, and God will give us the strength to get up and will lead us to life in all its fullness.

The lyrics of a song, written by Paul Francis Webster and first shared in the motion picture, "The Student Prince," in 1954, are appropriate words for our walks:

> I'll walk with God
> From this day on.
> His helping hand I'll lean upon.
> This is my prayer, my humble plea,
> May the Lord be ever with me.

Chapter 14

TURN ON THE RADIO

When we lived in the row house with the marble steps, we did not own a television. The radio was a source of information, music, and entertainment. I remember the names of some of the shows. They included "Fibber McGee and Molly," "The Shadow," "Our Miss Brooks," "Amos 'n' Andy," "Red Ryder," "Gunsmoke," and "The Lone Ranger."

"The Lone Ranger" was my favorite show. I pictured the scenes in my mind. I imagined the Lone Ranger and his friend, Tonto, fighting the outlaws and helping the citizens of towns to restore order and peace to their lives. I listened as they victoriously rode their horses, "Silver" and "Scout" out of town, and the Lone Ranger shouted, "Hi-yo, Silver! Away!" The people often wondered about the identity of that "masked man." He never remained in a place long enough for the citizens to thank him for his help. Sometimes, carrying a toy six shooter, riding a broom-stick horse, and fighting the bad guys, I attempted to play the role of that western hero.

Those radio shows awakened in me an appreciation for stories.

That appreciation grew when some of my relatives shared stories about their experiences in the past and about family members who had died and were influential. I sat and listened and was fascinated by their descriptions.

Also, I heard and learned stories from the Bible. I focused on the adventures of characters such as Abraham, Joseph, Moses, David, Ruth, Jeremiah, the twelve disciples of Jesus, and Paul. Through the years, I have learned more about their strengths and weaknesses and have been able to identify with them as fellow human beings.

Most significantly, I have been in awe of the greatest story- the story of Jesus. His birth, growth, life, ministry, teachings, suffering, death, and resurrection. As part of that story, Jesus shared many parables. Those stories are thought-provoking and reveal truth about relationships with God and relationships with one another. Some of those parables include, "The Prodigal Son" (Luke 15: 11-32), "The Good Samaritan" (Luke 10: 25-37), "The Sower and the Soils" (Mark 4: 1-9), and "The Talents"

(Matthew 25: 14-30). The parables are vivid and poignant and have evoked various responses from people through the years. Some persons have been offended by them; other persons have failed to grasp any significance from those stories; and others have read and heard them so often that familiarity has prevented any serious attention to the details. Everyone needs to return to the parables and prayerfully consider their meaning and purpose. Thereby, a new perspective can provide us with fresh truth for living.

When we are touched by the story of Jesus and sense his presence in us and with us, we can be inspired to realize and share our own faith-stories through words and actions. The apostle Paul's story is repeated three times in different situations in the book of Acts (Acts 9, Acts 22, and Acts 26). Every follower of Jesus Christ has a story to tell. Other needy individuals are waiting for and listening to those broadcasts.

Chapter 15

GOT MILK?

In my early years, I never lacked cold milk or good food. Periodically, a man came to our house and delivered milk. He placed the milk bottles on the top marble step, which was next to the front door. My parents then carried the bottles to the ice box in the kitchen, so that the milk did not spoil and remained cool. Also, a man regularly delivered a block of ice. He climbed the marble steps and went to the kitchen where he placed the block of ice in our ice box. The ice helped to preserve our food.

Before every meal, I was taught to pray, "God is great. God is good. Let us thank Him for our food. By His hands we all are fed. Give us, Lord, our daily bread." It was important for me to learn that truth first and then learn to thank the milk man and the ice man for their help. The Creator God is indeed the basic Source of those daily blessings.

A poem, attributed to M.D. Babcock emphasizes that truth:

Back of the bread is the snowy flour,
And back of the flour the mill,
And back of the mill is the wheat and the shower,
And the sun and the Father's will.

God the Creator provides for our basic needs, and we should never fail to express our gratitude to Him for His goodness to us. We are dependent on Him for our material and physical needs.

Jesus showed us God's divine concern for our well-being. On one occasion, he was teaching, and a large crowd of people had gathered to listen. He recognized that they had not eaten and were hungry. He then arranged for all of them to be fed, and they ate as much as they wanted. There were twelve baskets of leftovers, which were gathered by the disciples, so that no food would be wasted (John 6: 1-15). That food was available for later needs.

In his "Sermon on the Mount," when Jesus taught his followers to pray, he revealed to us the Holy God, Who cares deeply and wants the best for our lives (Matthew 6: 7-15). The Father God knows what we need even before we ask Him.

When we pray, "Give us this day our daily bread" (Verse 11, RSV), we can be assured that He hears and provides "sustaining bread" (Clarence Jordan's Translation).
Furthermore, this prayer is not merely a selfish request, but the word "us" indicates it is also a prayer for our fellow human beings. We are then inspired to do what we can to help provide "bread" for those who are poor. In that way, through us, they also will recognize that the Father God cares deeply about them and is the ultimate Source of those provisions.

Remembering the milk man and the ice man and my childhood prayer of thanks at the table, I trust that I will never take for granted the blessings set before me.

Chapter 16

A SPECIAL COLORING BOOK

Books have always been an important part of my life. When I was a toddler and a preschooler, my parents would read to me, and their wisdom in taking the time to do that, was the origin of my love for and appreciation of books.

In school, I began reading about "Dick, Jane, and Spot." Through the years, I have received books as gifts on birthdays and at Christmas. Also, I have enjoyed browsing in bookstores and libraries.

The Bible is the book that has been central in my life. Bibles have been presented to me in churches and have been given to me by family members at significant times.

When our family lived in the row house with the white marble steps at the front, my parents gave me my first Bible. It was Christmas 1945, and I was four months old. I still have that special book in my library. The leather cover is now worn and torn, and as I look through it, I see pictures on which I focused and from which I learned the stories in the Old and New

Testaments. Those pictures included: "The Return of the Dove" (Genesis 8:11); "Jonathan's warning to David" (1 Samuel 20:35); "The Vision of Isaiah" (Isaiah 1:1); "No Room in the Inn" (Luke 2:7); "The Raising of Jairus' Daughter" (Mark 5:4); and "Philip and the Man of Ethiopia" (Acts 8:27).

The title page is the most prominent to me now, because on that page I had taken a green crayon and scribbled all over it. I do not know what I was trying to communicate. There are several possibilities.

When I used crayons to color pictures in a coloring book, I had difficulty staying within the lines on the pages. Perhaps I was saying in my first Bible that I knew I would frequently live outside the lines of Biblical teachings. "Sin" is the "grown-up" term. I learned later that God could and would erase my mistakes and give me a clean page. On my part, I needed to go to Him, ask for His help, and try to do better. "Forgiveness" is the "grown-up" term.

Another possibility for my scribbling with that green crayon could be that I was trying to write my name in my first Bible. Through the years, I have been able to write my name in many places in the Biblical accounts.

For example, David's prayer in Psalm 51:10 is often my prayer, "Create in me a clean heart, O God, and put a new and right spirit within me." Peter's confession of faith in Jesus in Matthew 16:16 is my confession of faith through my many questions and doubts, "You are the Christ, the Son of the living God." I can identify with Timothy when Paul wrote to encourage him in 2 Timothy 1:5, "I am reminded of your sincere faith, a faith that dwelt first in your grandmother Lois and your mother Eunice and now, I am sure, dwells in you."

I wish I still had that green crayon, because I certainly have more coloring to do in that special book, called the Bible.

Chapter 17

FIRST NAME

Solomon shared some of his wisdom when he declared, "A good name is to be chosen rather than great riches" (Proverbs 22: 1a). Names are valuable gifts. When we are born into this world, we are given a name.

When I was born, my parents gave me the gift of a good name that is filled with meaning and family history: "Winter Rand Forder." "Winter" was my father's middle name, "Ralph Winter Forder." That was the maiden name of his mother, my grandmother, "Mary Frances Winter." My father's father, my grandfather, was named "Ralph Waldo Forder." He was named for "Ralph Waldo Emerson," writer, speaker, and philosopher, who lived in Boston in the nineteenth century. My middle name, "Rand," was my mother's maiden name, "Mary Ellen Rand." Her father, my grandfather, "Louis Albert Rand," had died before I was born. His wife, "Mary Moorehead Rand," my grandmother, often told me that I resemble him in many ways.

I do have a good name that I need to treasure, and I am in the process of attempting to live according to this truth, "To whom much is given, much is required" (Luke 12: 48).

When we lived in the brick house with the white marble steps at the front, I was called "Randy." That is the first name with which I identified. Relatives, church friends, playmates, and acquaintances called me by that first name. As I grew older, moved through the grades at school, and at the present time, I am referred to as "Rand." Many business and legal forms list my name as "Winter." Even now, though, when I am in a crowd of people, and someone calls to another person, "Randy," I automatically turn in the direction of that exchange when I hear my first name.

As I reflect on the different names which I am called, I notice that names are sometimes changed to indicate a new stage in life or to emphasize a religious belief.

In the Bible, we can find instances of God changing the names of persons who became heroes of the faith. For example, God called "Abram," which means "exalted father," to leave his home and family and promised to lead him to another land and bless him, so that he would be a blessing. Abram obeyed God, and when he was ninety-nine years old, God changed his name to "Abraham," which means "father of a multitude." God then established a covenant with him (Genesis 17: 4-5).

Jacob, "the supplanter" or "deceiver," stole the family blessing from his brother Esau. After his wrestling match at Peniel, God changed his name to "Israel," meaning "one who struggles with God" (Genesis 32: 28). Through that struggle, he received a blessing.

Saul was named after Israel's first king. With all his religious credentials, he was zealous in persecuting the followers of Jesus. After his encounter with the risen Jesus on the road to Damascus, his life was changed. His first name, "Saul," then became "Paul," the committed apostle (Acts 9: 1-9; Acts 13: 9).

There is one name that stands out from every other name (Philippians 2: 9). When Jesus was born, Joseph obeyed God's messenger, appearing to him in a dream, and gave that baby the name, "Jesus," because "he will save his people from their sins" (Matthew 1: 21). "Jesus" means Savior, and Jesus is the Savior. That was his first, last, and forever name. That name continues to inspire persons to worship and serve him.

Through faith in him, the way is open for us to become "children of God" (John 1: 12). Having been created in the "image of God" (Genesis 1: 27), we are given our very first name.

First names are not to be dismissed. With God's intervention, those names can lead us forward to life in all its fullness.

Chapter 18

A CORNER OF THE WORLD

Six-Hundred Ten Dukeland Street, in the city of Baltimore, Maryland, was the location of our row house with the white marble steps at the front. My world consisted of Dukeland Street, Edmondson Avenue, Poplar Grove Avenue, and Harlem Avenue. I walked with my family along those sidewalks. Many of our relatives even lived within that area.

I was not allowed to cross the streets by myself and always held my mother's hand or my father's hand when we did cross streets.

The story is told of the young boy who became angry with his parents and decided to run away from home. He got his red wagon and filled it with a blanket, his teddy bear, some candy, a bottle of juice, and his toothbrush. He then began his journey by pulling the wagon behind him. Looking back, he walked away from his house and circled the block many times. Finally, a police officer approached him and asked him about his actions. The boy told him that he was running away from home. The officer smiled and explained, "Wait a minute, you just keep walking around the block." The little fellow burst into tears and replied, "I know, but I'm not allowed to cross the streets." I wasn't allowed to cross the streets in our neighborhood, so my corner of the world consisted of the limited area I have described.

Sometimes we ventured outside of that space though. We rode the streetcar to downtown Baltimore, and I was in awe of the sights and sounds there. Sometimes we rode the streetcar which took us on Edmondson Avenue to visit family members on Lyndhurst Street and Eversley Street. There were also times when we rode in automobiles to church or to family gatherings.

Even though I experienced those outings, I became accustomed to my little corner of the world. I felt safe and secure as I rode my tricycle and little "hot rod" on the sidewalks in our neighborhood.

In our lives we need comfort zones where we can feel at home, can relate to people we know and trust, can rest, renew our spirits, and pray. However, we also need times when we cross those familiar boundaries to meet other persons and learn and grow and care and struggle and break old habits and deal with prejudice.

I have a map of Palestine in the time of Jesus and can view the area he knew well. In the Gospels, we can read about his birth in Bethlehem, his growing-up years in Nazareth, his baptism in the Jordan River, his teaching and preaching and ministering in the regions of Judea, Samaria, and Galilee. Also, we can learn about the risks he took by crossing geographical and societal boundaries.

For example, at Sychar, a city in Samaria, he, a Jewish male, asked a Samaritan woman for a drink of water at Jacob's well. That action was startling, because the Samaritan people and the Jewish people were bitter enemies. Furthermore, women were considered "second-class" citizens and were not worthy enough to engage in conversations with men. In the encounter, Jesus crossed lines established by hatred and prejudice (John 4).

Later, it was outside the Holy City of Jerusalem in Judea that Jesus was crucified and died. The writer of Hebrews states, "So Jesus also suffered outside the gate ... " (13: 12). Jesus did not remain within the false expectations of the crowd. The people wanted a King with military power for their Messiah, but Jesus the Christ, the Anointed One of God, proved to be a Suffering Servant.

We should express gratitude for those comfort zones where we need to live. However, we should also thank God for the courage and strength to step beyond our little corners of the world in the pursuit of truth, justice, and love. As we do so, we are following in the footsteps of Jesus, who is with us always.

Chapter 19

RIDE ALONG

My Family and I walked to stores, relatives' houses, and streetcar stops. As we walked, I was fascinated by the various models of automobiles. I learned quickly to identify Fords, Buicks, Chevrolets, and Pontiacs. I noticed Studebakers and DeSotos. My grandfather drove a Nash, in which I often rode.

I owned two favorite vehicles. I enjoyed riding my tricycle on the sidewalk in front of the white marble steps of our row house. I fell off my bike once and hurt my knee. My parents, who were always there with me, helped me to dry the tears and put medicine and a bandage on the painful scratch. That fall, though, did not deter me from continuing to speed along.

My other vehicle was my "hot rod." It was red, with a white strip on the hood and a horn on the side. I waved to my parents and our neighbors as I pedaled along the sidewalk. How proud I was to display my fancy car.

Jesus walked along the roads of Palestine. Mark's Gospel describes his active pace. As he walked throughout the region of Galilee, he preached in synagogues and cast out demons. He healed a leper who had approached him and asked for his help. In Capernaum, he healed a paralyzed man. He went about doing good! (Mark, chapters 1 and 2).

In addition to Jesus' walking, Mark's Gospel describes Jesus' riding in a boat with his disciples on the Sea of Galilee. A severe storm frightened the disciples, and they awoke Jesus, who had been sleeping. They wondered if he cared about them in such a crisis. He commanded the wind to stop and ordered the sea to calm down, "Peace! Be Still!" (Mark 4: 39). He pointed out to his men the significance of faith in times of fear. The disciples marveled at his power and his identity. The boat then moved safely to the other side of the sea.

In Mark's Gospel (chapter 6), we read that Jesus had been teaching a crowd of people. He saw that they were hungry, and he then provided food for them to eat. He told his disciples to take the boat and to meet him on the other side of the sea in Bethsaida. He dismissed the crowd and went into the hills to pray. Early in the morning, he saw that his men were in trouble on the turbulent sea. He walked to the water and then walked on the sea to them. When the disciples saw a figure walking on the water, they were terrified, because they thought it was a ghost. Jesus spoke to them, "Take heart, it is I; have no fear" (Mark 6: 50). He got into the boat with them. The wind calmed down, and the disciples were amazed.

Walking or riding, in calm or stormy weather, filled with fear and uncertainty, we today can be assured that Jesus Christ, the living Lord, is always with us and for us. He shares with us the ever-present love of God, and nothing can separate us from God's love (Romans 8: 37-39). That love is revealed most completely in and through and beyond the cross.

Jesus walked toward the city of Jerusalem and the cross. However, he rode into the city on a colt, borrowed from a nearby village (Mark 11: 1-10). That royal entry on a donkey should have awakened the people to the identity of Jesus. He was not a political king riding on a white horse to proclaim a military victory, but the humble king of peace and love, whom the prophet Zechariah had described (Zechariah 9:9).

G.K. Chesterton imagined that on the ride along into Jerusalem, even the donkey was affirmed by the presence of Jesus. Chesterton wrote the poem entitled, "The Donkey":

> When fishes flew and forests walked
> And figs grew upon thorns,
> Some moment when the moon was blood
> Then surely I was born:
> With monstrous head and sickening cry
> And ears like errant wings,
> The devil's walking parody
> On all four-footed things;
> The tattered outlaw of the earth
> Of ancient crooked will:
> Starve, scourge, deride me: I am dumb,
> I keep my secret still.
> Fools! For I also had my hour;

One far fierce hour and sweet:
There was a shout about my ears,
And palms before my feet.[4]

---

[4] Caroline Miles Hill, ed., <u>The World's Great Religious Poetry</u>,
(New York: The Macmillan Company, 1924), p. 268.

Chapter 20

THE WORKER

The row house with the white marble steps at the front was narrow with three rooms on the first floor. The dining room was in the center with the kitchen at the back and the living room at the front.

My parents decided to have wallpaper put on the walls in the dining room. A man came to look at the room, estimated the cost, and said that he would do the job for them.

When he came to work on the room, I was interested in the project. I watched and was fascinated as he measured, cut the wallpaper, spread paste on the back of the sheets of paper, and then positioned them on the wall. He made certain that the wallpaper fit properly. He was always patient with me, a little boy who was "glued" to his labor for several days. When he finished, he examined his work with pride, and my parents were delighted with the job.

I continue to be amazed at the skills of some individuals. They are gifted people, who have learned a trade and can do their work well. It is inspiring to witness skilled workers take pride in their accomplishments.

In the Bible, we can read about skilled workers. King Solomon drafted thousands of workers to build the temple. There were stone cutters and those who cut down trees and then prepared the timber for the structure. It took seven years to build the temple. (1 Kings, chapters 5 and 6).

The apostle Paul worked as a tentmaker. In the city of Corinth, he met Aquila and Priscilla, who were also tentmakers. He stayed with them and worked with them. (Acts 18: 1-4). With that trade in mind, he taught Timothy to be a worker for Christ. He was interested in Timothy becoming approved by God and taking pride in his work. That involved "rightly handling" God's message. (2 Timothy 2: 15). The phrase, "rightly handling" was based on the picture of the tentmaker "cutting straight" animal skins used to make the tents.

Jesus was referred to as a carpenter. When he visited his home town, taught in the synagogue, and performed miracles, the people of Nazareth were amazed and questioned, "Isn't this the carpenter?" (Mark 6: 3). As a boy, spending time in Joseph's shop, Jesus learned the trade. Later in his teaching, Jesus used illustrations from the carpenter's world of work. For example, he knew about working on wooden yokes and fitting them properly on animals. In his teaching, he invited us to put on his yoke, which would provide us with rest and not more heavy loads. When we link our lives with him, our burdens are shared and become lighter. The rest we then experience can give us the strength to move forward.

Reflecting on God coming to live and work with us in the person of Jesus Christ, G.A. Studdert-Kennedy wrote the poem entitled, "It's Hard To Be A Carpenter":

> I wonder what He charged for chairs
> At Nazareth.
> And did men try to beat Him down,
> And boast about it in the town,
> "I bought it cheap for half a crown
> From that mad carpenter"?
> And did they promise and not pay,
> Put it off to another day,
> O did they break His heart that way,
> My Lord the Carpenter?
> I wonder did He know my fears and frets?
> The Gospel writer here forgets
> To tell about the Carpenter.

But that's just what I want to know.
Ah! Christ in glory, here below
Men cheat and lie to one another so
It's hard to be a carpenter.[5]

As we follow "the Master Carpenter," we are to be more than spectators, watching in amazement as his work proceeds. "We are partners working together for God" (1 Corinthians 3: 9a, GNT). As we participate with other followers, we can learn to become skilled workers for his cause.

---

[5] G.A. Studdert-Kennedy, The Best of G.A. Studdert-Kennedy, "Selected from his writings by a friend," (New York: Harper & Brothers,1924), pp. 158-159).

Chapter 21

THE OLD LADY

She "invaded" our home. When she walked in the front door of the row house with the white marble steps at the front, I was afraid of the stranger.

She was older than my parents and my grandmother and walked with difficulty. I turned away when she approached and tried to hug me. I learned that she was my great-grandmother, the mother of my grandfather who died before I was born. The plan was for her to visit with us for several days.

"Grandma Rand" was the name she was called, and she became the center of attention for the family. I was jealous because I had always held that spot. One day, she tried to make friends with me by offering me an apple. I reluctantly accepted and was prompted by my mother to say, "Thank you." I thought of the story about "Snow White and the Seven Dwarfs." I remembered that the wicked witch gave Snow White a poison apple, and I never did eat that apple. I was relieved and happy when my great-grandmother said, "Goodbye."

As I became older, I learned more about my great-grandmother, Margaret Rand. I have discovered that she was an intelligent woman, who always claimed that she was related to Woodrow Wilson. She loved the city of Washington, D.C., and she and her husband, Louis Rand, owned an apartment building on Florida Avenue in that city. She was never reluctant to share her convictions. From all that I have learned, I picture her as a trailblazer in her time. As a boy, relating to my great-grandmother, I revealed some tendencies that, unfortunately, can plague us throughout our lives.

In his teaching, Jesus warned about childishness. He pointed to children playing in the marketplace. Some were whining and complaining because other children would not participate in the games they had planned (Matthew 11: 16-17). Adults sometimes whine and complain because they do not get their way. At any age, selfishness can lead to harmful results.

For example, Saul, the first king of Israel, began his reign with great promise and potential. However, he became so absorbed in his jealousy of David, that Saul's life and reign ended tragically (1 Samuel 19: 8-10; 31: 4).

In contrast, Jesus emphasized childlikeness when his disciples were questioning him about greatness and who could be first in the kingdom of heaven. He called a child to stand in front of the group. As they looked at the child, Jesus said," Truly, I say to you, unless you turn and become like children, you will never enter the kingdom of heaven. Whoever humbles himself like this child, he is the greatest in the kingdom of heaven" (Matthew 18: 1-4). Characterized by dependence and trust, children can teach us essential truths in our relationship with God. Jesus later showed the disciples what he meant when he refused a political crown and suffered and died on a cross.

As I continue to grow in my relationship with God, three things I pray. First, I pray for God's help as I seek to leave behind my childish ways. As Paul wrote to the Christian community in Corinth, "When I was a child, I spoke like a child, I thought like a child, I reasoned like a child; but

when I became a man, I gave up childish ways"
(1 Corinthians 13: 11).

Also, I pray that I will become more childlike.
That is only possible through my dependence
on and trust in Jesus Christ. John declares in his
Gospel, "And to all who received him, who
believed in his name, he gave power to become
children of God" (John 1: 12).

Finally, my prayer is that my wise great-
grandmother, with her years of experience,
understood my childish behavior and forgave
me. I regret that I never had the opportunity to
apologize to her.

Chapter 22

A FRIEND FROM OKLAHOMA

I remember my parents gathering clothes, books, and other items to send to a person named Dr. Frank Belvin. They told me that he lived in a place called Oklahoma and that he was a medical doctor who served as a missionary to the Indian people there. He himself was an Indian who grew up on a reservation. "Indian" was the term used in the early 1950's instead of "Native American." At my age I knew about conflicts between cowboys and Indians, and the Indians were always the "bad guys."

One Sunday, Dr. Belvin came from Oklahoma to be the guest speaker at our church. I was curious about seeing an Indian in person. When he began the sermon, he was not what I had expected. He looked, dressed, and sounded the same as every man in our congregation.

I usually sat next to my cousin in church. We laughed, made silly noises, and drew pictures on the Sunday bulletin. We were often reprimanded by our parents and were made to sit at opposite ends of the church pew. That Sunday, though, our behavior was different. We listened, and I was fascinated by Dr. Belvin's story. He told about growing up on an Indian reservation, and he described how he had been changed when Jesus came into his life. After his training, he went back to Oklahoma to care for his people there. They needed to be set free from poverty, alcoholism, and violence. He knew from his own personal experience that his people needed to encounter the liberating power of Jesus Christ. He dedicated his life to making Christ known to them. Even at my young age, I sensed the genuine, powerful message he shared with us that day.

After Dr. Belvin's visit to our church, my parents continued to send items to him for his important work. One day, the mailman came to our row house, walked up the marble steps, rang the doorbell, and handed my mother a package. In the package was a red paperback book from Dr. Belvin. My parents read the title, Warhorse: Along the Jesus Road. I learned that the book described Dr. Belvin's life and ministry.

Since that childhood meeting with the friend from Oklahoma, my respect for Native Americans has grown far beyond the "Cowboy-

Indian" level. They have contributed so much to our society. When I was in school, I read the biography of Jim Thorpe. He was an outstanding athlete and the first Native American to win a gold medal in the Olympics. Also, during wartime, Native Americans served our country as "code talkers," who used their tribal languages to transmit coded messages.

As Christians join with other Christians of different backgrounds "along the Jesus road," there is a bond that remains secure. The Christian journey is often difficult. We still deal with prejudice and wrong attitudes, and our lives are still filled with shortcomings. On that life-long adventure, though, we share the road with Christ, who forgives us, provides us with inner resources, and creates fellowship.

In the book of Acts, Luke tells the story of the early church. He mentions that followers of Jesus were often referred to as the "Way" (Acts 9:2; 19:9,23; 24:22). Even their enemies noticed that on the everyday road of life, the "Jesus crowd" acted and reacted in a different manner. A love and compassion was visible in their lives.

As we share the road with other followers of Jesus, we can often recognize the presence of the risen, living Christ, who promised, "I am with you always, to the close of the age" (Matthew 28:20b).

Chapter 23

SMALL MATTERS

I remember that my grandmother stayed at home with me when my parents needed to shop in our community for groceries or other items. Sometimes as they walked home, they stopped at McComas' Pharmacy on Poplar Grove Street and brought my grandmother and me some ice cream from the pharmacy. At that time, drug stores, as they were called, had a lunch counter where customers could sit on stools and order sodas, milk shakes, sundaes, sandwiches, or other food.

I watched and waited for my parents to walk up the white marble steps of our row house. I looked forward to a small dixie cup containing one scoop of vanilla ice cream. That little cup of ice cream brought a smile to my face and happiness to my day. As a four-year-old boy, I celebrated with that small gift.

Little things can mean a lot. Consider a smile which can brighten the whole day for someone else. Consider one small act of kindness which can lead to many other acts of kindness.

In contrast, though, little things can also lead to negative results. For example, one word can encourage or compliment or congratulate. However, one word can also damage or destroy a relationship.

In that regard, James, a leader in the early church, shared a warning in his New Testament letter. He described in vivid terms the manner in which we use our small tongues. He explained, "We use it to give thanks to our Lord and Father and also to curse other people, who are created in the likeness of God. Words of thanksgiving and cursing pour out from the same mouth. My friends, this should not happen!" (James 3: 9-10, GNT). That little tongue can present big challenges.

When God chose the right time to come and be with us on this earth, He came, not as some enormous creature from outer space, but as a tiny baby, named "Jesus," who was born in a manger. That "one solitary life" introduced us to God's love for us, our need to love God and one another, showed us the way to meaning and purpose in everyday living, and changed for the best the course of this world in which we live. Jesus revealed the truth that little things can and should result in the fulfillment of life.

On one occasion when Jesus' disciples were unable to heal an epileptic boy, Jesus noticed a mustard seed, which was the smallest seed of all. He told his followers that even if their faith was as small as that seed, they could deal successfully with large obstacles or difficulties, which might appear to them as huge mountains (Matthew 17: 20).

In the Gospel of John, we read about the time when Jesus, with a little boy's lunch, consisting of just five barley loaves and two fish, fed a large crowd of more than five thousand people (John 6: 1-14).

Whenever I participate in the Lord's Supper in our church, I take a small piece of bread and a little cup filled with grape juice. Those small symbols, which I can hold in my hands, represent his broken body and his blood, poured out for the forgiveness of sins. It was indeed a huge sacrifice as he suffered and died on that cross. He created a new covenant in which God's love is far-reaching and unconditional. He made possible a pathway to salvation for us. (1 Corinthians 11: 23-29; Mark 14: 22-25; Matthew 26: 26-29; Luke 22: 14-20).

The little dixie cup with one scoop of ice cream appears to be a small matter, but it proved to be, for me, the beginning of recognizing large gifts contained in small forms that hold ultimate significance.

Chapter 24

THE SOUND OF MUSIC

The row house with the white marble steps was often filled with the sound of music. My mother was an excellent pianist, and my father loved to sing. They both were involved in the music ministry of several churches throughout their lives. I remember listening to my mother playing hymns and my father singing along. Early in my life I became familiar with the tunes and the words.

Our church was also filled with the sound of music. Members of our extended family directed the choir, sang in the choir, sang solos, led the congregation in singing, and played the organ and the piano. As soon as I was old enough, I became a member of the children's choir.

Bibles and hymn books were always available in the pew racks in the sanctuary of our church. Those two books were important as members of our congregation worshiped God. Both books told me the story of Jesus.

The sound of music can be heard throughout the Bible. Many composers have listened. For example, George Friderick Handel heard the sound and composed the oratorio, "The Messiah," in 1741. That masterpiece is composed of three parts: the birth of Jesus, the death of Jesus, and the resurrection of Jesus.

In the Old Testament, the sound of music can be heard especially in the book of Psalms. It is considered to be the hymn book of God's people. Many of the Psalms are attributed to David. David was a musician who played the harp to help King Saul whenever the king needed a soothing sound to quiet his troubled life (1 Samuel 16: 23). It has been said that David wrote seventy-three of the Psalms. For example, King David wrote this song of praise, "I will extol thee, my God and King, and bless thy name for ever and ever. Every day I will bless thee, and praise thy name for ever and ever. Great is the Lord, and greatly to be praised, and his greatness is unsearchable" (Psalm 145: 1-3).

King David appointed priests to sing praises in the house of the Lord. Asaph was appointed as the leader of those musicians. Psalm 75 is one of the songs which was ascribed to Asaph, "We give thanks to thee, O God; we call on thy name and recount thy wondrous deeds" (verse 1).

In the New Testament, the sound of music surrounded the birth of Jesus. Luke's Gospel mentions several songs: Mary's song of faith and praise (Luke 1: 46-55); the song of Zechariah, John's father (Luke 1: 68-79); the Angels' song of praises to God, as the amazed shepherds listened (Luke 2: 13-14); and Simeon's song in the Temple, as he held the infant in his arms and thanked God for the Lord's promised Messiah.

In the Apostle Paul's letter to the Philippian church, his words in Philippians 2: 5-11 have often been referred to as a hymn. The hymn describes Jesus' pre-existence, his earthly ministry, and his glorification, and the song especially emphasizes his humility.

Whenever I now sing familiar hymns such as, "O Little Town of Bethlehem," "What a Friend We Have in Jesus," "O, Master, Let Me Walk with Thee," "Leaning on the Everlasting Arms," "When I Survey the Wondrous Cross," "He Lives," and many others, I am inspired to renew my faith commitment to Christ.

Since childhood, music has been a vital part of my life and faith. Using child-like imagination, I can think about the white marble steps singing and the sound of music still being heard on Dukeland Street.

Chapter 25

TRAINS, PLANES, AND GRANDPARENTS

My grandmother would hold my hand as we walked down the marble steps of the house. There were no railings to hold, so it would have been easy to fall. We then walked about five blocks, sat on a stone wall, and watched trains pass by. I was fascinated by the engines, the different types of cars, and the red caboose at the end of each train. Since those early years, I have been a passenger on many trains and have met family members at train stations in many locations.

Trains are not as awesome to me now as they were in my preschool years. However, I think that one of the reasons I now have a Lionel train layout in our home is to somehow recover some of those childhood memories.

As my grandmother and I walked back home, I would sometimes stand still when I heard the sound of an airplane flying above. I would look up and watch that plane until it was out of sight.

Since those early years, I have been a passenger many times on aircrafts, and I have spent hours waiting for flights. Also, I have waited at airports for family members and friends to arrive or depart. Watching planes is not as amazing to me now as it was during my preschool years. It seems that I have lost the sense of wonder I experienced as a child.

Now, as a grandparent, I am in awe of my young grandchildren. They are indeed personal gifts from God to our family. Recently, as I have watched them, I have been awakened to my need to recover an awareness of the marvels around me. I have seen them paying attention to a caterpillar crawling across the lawn, or a flower blooming in the garden, or two squirrels chasing each other up a tree, or a brightly-colored bird lighting on a feeder to eat seed.

I am reminded of a Psalm of David in which he praises God, "O Lord, our Lord, your greatness is seen in all the world! Your praise reaches up to the heavens; it is sung by children and babies" (Psalm 51:1-2a, GNT).

Learning from my grandchildren about marveling, I am beginning to realize anew the wonder of the persons who surround my life.

Jesus always seemed to exhibit such wonder as he related to individuals. For example, a rich, young man ran up to Jesus and asked him, "What must I do to inherit eternal life?" As a conversation ensued, "Jesus looking upon him loved him" (Mark 10: 17-22). It has been said that "God loves each one of us just as if there were only one of us to love." Jesus came to reveal the unconditional love of God.

That brings me back to my grandmother. My cousin and I called her "Nana." And as I think of her now, I recognize that she was a "wonder woman." Born in 1887, she survived a case of the Spanish flu in 1918. She lived through the Great Depression era. Her husband died of ALS in 1934 at the age of forty-seven. She and her two teenage daughters continued to move forward. She worked as an employee at an elementary school cafeteria in Baltimore and was admired by her co-workers. I remember her as one who was devoted to her family. And her love for her two grandsons was never failing. I appreciated her sense of humor and was impressed by her inner strength. At her funeral service in 1967, her pastor called her, "a woman of quiet faith," and I continue to be in awe of that faith.

The apostle Paul wrote to Timothy, "I am reminded of your sincere faith, a faith that dwelt first in your grandmother Lois and your mother Eunice and now, I am sure, dwells in you" (2 Timothy 1:5, RSV). When my grandchildren remember me, it is my prayer that they will be amazed at the "quiet faith" which I am attempting to cultivate.

EPILOGUE

As I have reflected on the early years of my life, the persons who have walked with me up and down the white marble steps have died. However, my relationships with them have continued to live. Their faith and values influence me in the present, and those special people inspire me now to live a life worthy of their legacy.

I think of the apostle Paul's words of advice in his personal letter to the Christians in Philippi : "In conclusion, my friends, fill your minds with those things that are good and deserve praise: things that are true, noble, right, pure, lovely, and honorable. Put into practice what you learned and received from me, both from my words and my actions. And the God who gives us peace will be with you" (Philippians 4: 8-9, GNT).

God in Jesus Christ has promised to be with us throughout our lives. "He says he is with us on our journeys. He says he has been with us since each of our journeys began. Listen for him.

Listen to the sweet and bitter airs of your present and your past for the sound of him."[6]

Writing these "Meditations," as I have experienced the discipline of listening for him in my past, I have discovered a new awareness of his presence in the "everydayishness" of my life now. I also believe "the sound of him" will continue into my future.

Through the good days and the bad days, with doubts and questions, may we all listen closely for the God of love, whose grace is sufficient from beginning to end.

---

[6] Frederick Buechner, <u>Listening to Your Life</u>, New York: Harper Collins, 1992), p. 5.

www.ingramcontent.com/pod-product-compliance
Lightning Source LLC
Chambersburg PA
CBHW071024120626
46546CB00003B/1202